SHARK
and other sea creatures
DICTIONARY

An A to Z of sea life

Author Clint Twist
Managing Editor Ruth Hooper
Designer Julia Harris
Production Nicolette Colborne
Consultant Zoologists Robert and Valerie Davies
Illustrators Robin Bouttell (Wildlife Arts Ltd), Robin Carter
(Wildlife Arts Ltd), Stuart Carter (Wildlife Arts Ltd), Sandra Doyle
(Wildlife Arts Ltd), Denys Ovenden, Gill Tomblin
Photograph credit (page 4/5) Jeff Rotman/naturepl.com

AN ANDROMEDA BOOK

Published in 2002 by
Andromeda Oxford Limited
11-13 The Vineyard
Abingdon
Oxon
OX14 3PX
United Kingdom
www.andromeda.co.uk

ISBN 1-861990-75-8

Printed in China by Dai Nippon Co. Ltd.

Size Comparison Pictures

Throughout this dictionary you will see a symbol,
either a hand or a diver, next to a red icon of each
creature listed. The hand or diver will help you to
imagine the size of each creature in real life.

18 cm

The first symbol is a human
adult's hand, which measures
about 18 cm (7 in.) from the
wrist to the tip of the longest
finger. Some creatures are
smaller than this, so the size
comparison will help you to
imagine their size.

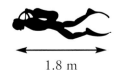

1.8 m

The second symbol is an adult
diver. He would measure about
1.8 m (6 ft.) from head to toe
in real life. The symbol will
help you to imagine the size of
some of the really big creatures
in this book.

SHARK
and other sea creatures
DICTIONARY
An A to Z of sea life

ANDROMEDA

Life in the sea

Sea animals, like land animals, can be divided into two groups – vertebrates (animals with a backbone) and invertebrates (animals that lack a backbone or other internal bones). Vertebrates in the sea include some mammals, very few reptiles and a great many fish. Sea mammals include whales, seals and sea lions. Fish come in an incredible variety of shapes and sizes. Sea reptiles are nearly all sea snakes.

Mammals and reptiles breathe air through lungs and those that live in the sea must come to the surface to breathe. Fish breathe by extracting oxygen from water through gills, and must remain underwater to survive.

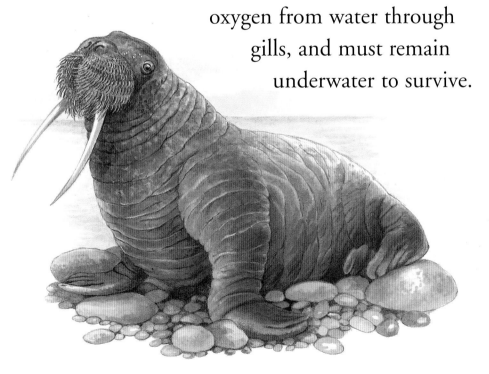

SHARKS
The shark family includes some of the largest fish in the world. Sharks' skeletons are made of cartilage instead of bone.

REPTILES
Nearly all the reptiles in the sea are snakes. There are about 40 different types of sea snake, specially adapted to live in the water.

RAYS

Rays are part of the
shark family. They
have fins that look
like wings, so it looks
as if they are flying in the water.

MAMMALS

Sea mammals must come to the surface to breathe
air. They include whales, seals, walruses, sea
lions, dolphins and porpoises.

INVERTEBRATES

Jellyfish, crabs, starfish,
sea urchins, octopi and
squid are all invertebrates
and there are many more.
Invertebrates do not have
a backbone.

BONY FISH

Unlike the shark family, bony fish
have a skeleton of hard bone.
There are over 20,000 species of
bony fish swimming in the seas.

Fish groups

There are two main groups of fish in the sea – bony fish (which make up the majority of fish) and the sharks and their relatives. Bony fish have a skeleton that is made of hard bone. Most bony fish have bodies that are covered with scales. They have soft fins with curving, bone-like reinforcements. A few bony fish, such as the eels, have skin rather than scales. Sharks have a skeleton that is made of cartilage, which is softer than bone, and their bodies are covered with a tough skin. A shark's skin also covers its fins and tail. Rays, with their eerie flapping 'wings', and the strange deep-sea chimaeras are related to sharks, and they also have skeletons made of cartilage.

Queensland grouper

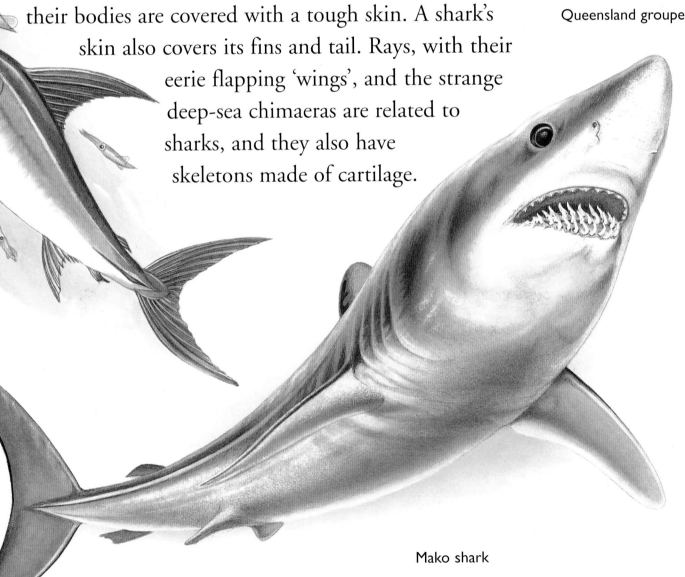

Swordfish

Mako shark

Invertebrates

There are many different invertebrates in the sea. Most live in or on the sea bottom, at all depths from the shoreline to very deep water.

Crustaceans have jointed legs and their bodies are covered by a tough outer shell. Crabs, shrimps, prawns and lobsters are all crustaceans. Some crustaceans have a much softer, more flexible shell than lobsters.

Echinoderms, such as sea urchins and starfish, have defensive spines. Starfish have flexible arms, while most urchins have a hard shell.

Molluscs are soft-bodied, often with a shell for protection. Molluscs with a pair of shells, like clams, are called bivalves. Gastropods are molluscs with just one shell, like snails. Squid, octopi and cuttlefish are another group of molluscs but they have flexible tentacles.

Cnidaria is the family name for all types of jellyfish, sea anemones and coral animals.

Worms are invertebrates with long, soft bodies, like the ribbonworm and the leech.

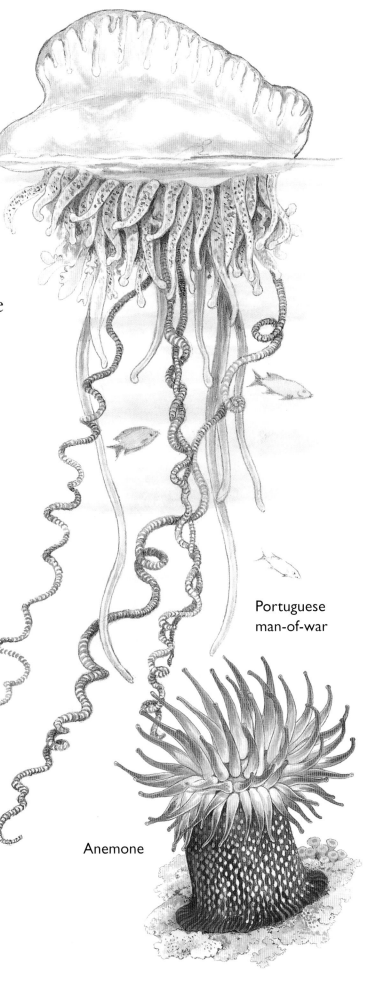

Portuguese man-of-war

Anemone

Ghost crab

7

Food and feeding

Many fish and other sea animals are meat-eating predators. Ocean plants are too small to provide enough food for large animals. The oceans are not a peaceful place for their inhabitants and there is a constant struggle between predator and prey. This struggle is fierce and it is fought with deadly weapons. Ocean predators are the most ferocious in the world.

Giant squid

Teeth

Most predators have teeth, and the big meat-eating sharks have the most fearsome teeth of all. Each tooth is roughly triangular in shape and has serrated edges with dozens of tiny, razor-sharp points. A shark's teeth can cut effortlessly through skin, muscle, and even bone. Sharks twist their bodies as they strike at prey, so they can slice off large chunks of flesh with each bite. Among mammals, the spiral horn of the narwhal and the tusks of the walrus are in fact greatly extended teeth.

Great white shark

Spines, stings and swords

Spines are everywhere under the sea – on the shells of urchins, in the fins of fish, and even under the skirts of the vampire squid. The porcupine fish combines spines with the ability to inflate its body, which makes it even harder for a predator to swallow. Most rays have a spine on their tails and jellyfish are armed with hundreds of tiny stinging cells. Some fish have a snout shaped like a sword or saw, which may be used as a weapon.

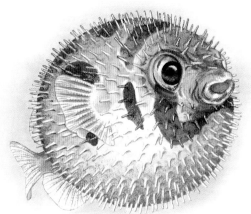

Porcupine fish

Blue-ringed octopus

Poison

Poison is a popular weapon under water. All of it is deadly to its intended victims, and much of it is also dangerous to humans. Many sea creatures defend themselves by flowing venom into their prey though special spines. Sea predators, such as the sea krait, the cone shell and the anemone use venom to immobilise or kill their prey.

Other weapons

All living animals produce tiny amounts of electrical current. A few rays can generate much greater amounts of electricity in special muscle cells. Other sea animals have even more exotic weapons. The slime eel can turn the water around it into thick, suffocating, jelly-like slime; and some sea cucumbers can squirt sticky, poisonous threads.

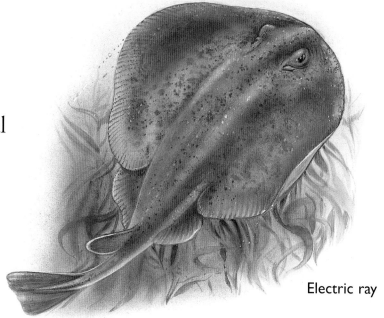

Electric ray

Aa

Anemone

The sea anemone is an animal that looks like an exotic underwater flower. Its petals are actually sticky tentacles with a poisonous sting. The anemone lives attached to a rock, or sometimes to a crab's shell. It feeds on shrimps and small fish, which it catches and pulls into its central mouth.

Max diameter: 90 cm (3 ft.)

Angelshark

Max length: 2.5 m (8 ft.)

The angelshark has a wide mouth ringed with needle-pointed teeth. It lives on the sea bottom where it hides buried in the sand. When fish or squid swim too close, its mouth opens and closes like a trap. The angelshark is not considered very dangerous, but it will give you a painful bite if provoked.

Anglerfish

The anglerfish has wide jaws, sharp teeth and a fleshy, dangling strand called a lure to attract prey. The lures of many deep-sea anglerfish have luminous tips that glow in the deep, dark water. The black anglerfish has an elastic stomach so it can swallow prey that is much larger than itself!

Max length: 1 m 20 cm (3 ft. 9 in.)

Barracuda

The great barracuda is a hunter of tropical waters. It feeds mainly on other fish, and attacks its prey at high speed with a snap of its powerful jaws. The barracuda sometimes attacks swimmers and divers. Its small but razor-sharp teeth can easily bite off a person's arm or leg.

Max length: 2 m (6 ft. 6 in.)

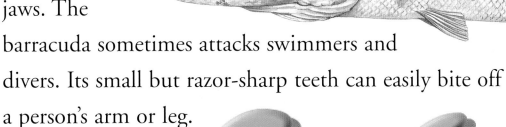

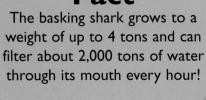

Fact

The basking shark grows to a weight of up to 4 tons and can filter about 2,000 tons of water through its mouth every hour!

Max length: 15 m (49 ft.)

Basking shark

The basking shark is the world's second largest fish. Its enormous bulk can capsize a small boat, but otherwise this giant shark is harmless. The basking shark has large jaws, but no teeth. It feeds by swimming with its mouth open, filtering shrimp and other small crustaceans from the water with its gills.

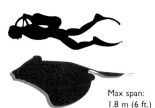

Bat ray

The bat ray lives on the sea bottom in shallow waters, where it spends most of its time resting. It feeds mainly on crustaceans and worms, which it grinds up with its blunt teeth. The bat ray has five short stinging spines near the base of its tail. The spines deter predators, and can also give people a painful wound if they try to handle the ray.

Max span: 1.8 m (6 ft.)

Max length: 1.3 m (4 ft. 3 in.)

Blind shark

The blind shark lives near rocky coasts and is sometimes found in tidal pools. The blind shark emerges at night to feed on invertebrates. Despite its name it is not blind, but it often looks that way because it rolls its eyes when frightened or caught.

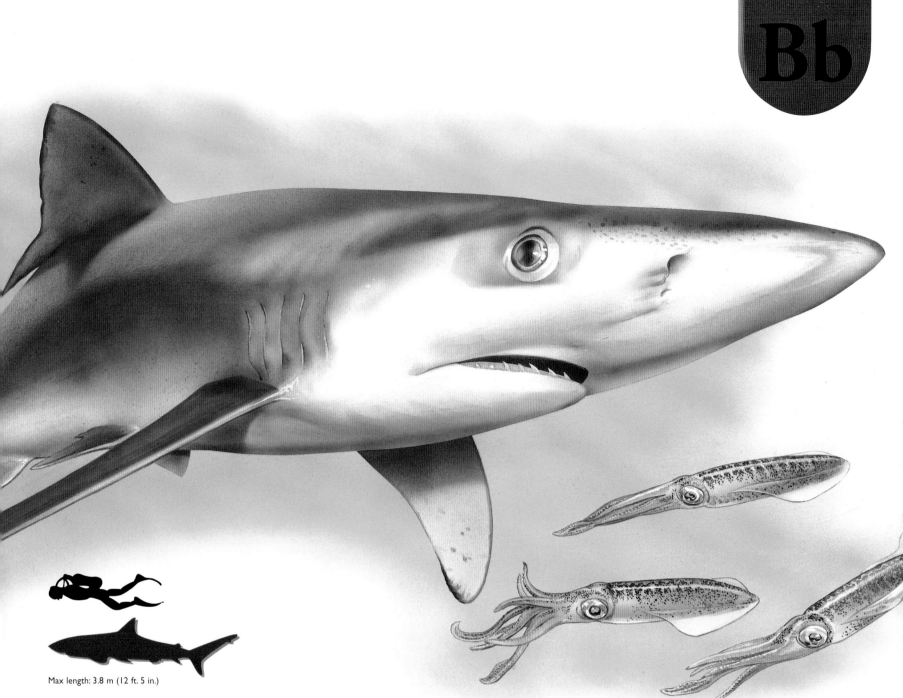

Max length: 3.8 m (12 ft. 5 in.)

Blue shark

The blue shark lives in the open ocean, but is sometimes found in coastal kelp beds. It is a large and vicious predator that feeds on squid and fish, which it consumes in large quantities. The blue shark is aggressive and dangerous, and will attack swimmers and divers without being provoked.

Fact

The upper body of the blue shark is dark blue and the underside is nearly white. Lots of sharks have colouring like this to camouflage them if they are seen from above or from below. This is called countershading.

Max length: 12.5 cm (5 in.)

Blue-ringed octopus

The blue-ringed octopus is a small, deadly animal that lives on coral reefs in the Indian and Pacific Oceans. It feeds on fish, which it catches in its eight tentacles and then kills with a venomous bite. The venom is powerful enough to kill a person in just 15 minutes. The bright blue markings warn predators (and divers) to stay away from this dangerous little octopus.

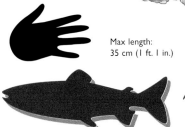

Max length:
35 cm (1 ft. 1 in.)

Bristlemouth

There are probably more bristlemouths in the world than any other type of fish, with tens of thousands of them at a time being caught in trawl nets. The bristlemouth gets its name from the fine teeth that line its mouth like the bristles of a brush. You are unlikely to encounter this fish while swimming, because it lives in very deep water.

Fact

The faint glow of light from the ocean's surface makes each fish visible as a silhouette to any predators lurking below. Some fish, such as the bristlemouths, can give off light so their silhouette cannot be seen.

Bronze whaler

Max length: 3 m (10 ft.)

The bronze whaler, with its distinctive colouring, is also known as the copper shark. It lives near rocky coasts and around islands. The bronze whaler feeds on a variety of small sharks, fish, rays, squid and even sea snakes. It is considered dangerous, and has been known to attack swimmers.

Bull shark

Max length: 3.5 m (11 ft. 5 in.)

The bull shark is probably the most dangerous shark in the world. It lives in coastal waters, but it can also tolerate fresh water. Bull sharks have been sighted in rivers a long way from the sea. This big, slow-moving shark will attack and eat just about anything, and it is responsible for many attacks on people.

Catshark

Max length: 75 cm (2 ft. 5 in.)

The catshark gets its name because its eyes look like a cat's eyes. This slow-moving shark lives in coastal waters and feeds at night on crustaceans and other invertebrates. The catshark sucks its prey into its mouth rather than biting with its teeth.

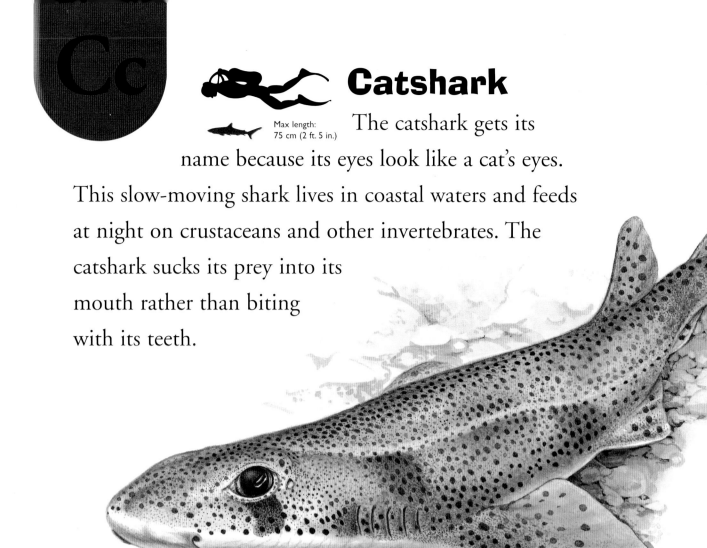

Chironex

Max length: 25 cm (10 in.)

Chironex is also known as the box jellyfish, or the sea wasp. It is found off the shores of Australia, and has a fearsome reputation for its agonizing and sometimes fatal sting. Chironex has a sting in its tentacles that can kill a person in minutes. During the season when sea wasps are plentiful, many Australian beaches are closed to swimmers.

Max length: 20 cm (8 in.)

Cone shell

The cone shell is a marine snail that lives on tropical reefs and shores. It can project its mouth forward like a dart to reach prey that has tried to escape into tight spaces in the rocks. The cone shell kills its prey by injecting nerve poison through its teeth. If you see one on the beach, don't pick it up or it could give you a nasty sting.

Fact

Some cone shells, such as the tulip cone, have been known to kill humans. Others, like the marble cone, can cause an unpleasant, although not fatal, sting.

Max length: 3 m (10 ft.)

Conger eel

The conger eel lives mainly around rocky coastlines. With powerful jaws and sharp teeth, it is a voracious hunter of fish, squid and crustaceans. The eel will not attack a person unless it is provoked, but divers should be careful. It likes to rest in caves and under rocks during the day. If disturbed, it can deliver a very nasty bite.

Cookiecutter shark

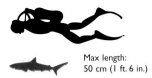

Max length:
50 cm (1 ft. 6 in.)

The cookiecutter shark has a unique method of attacking creatures much larger than itself. It has lips shaped like a suction cup and razor-sharp, triangular teeth. The shark bites into the side of its victim and, using its suction lips to remain attached, rotates its whole body. The lower teeth, which are much bigger than the upper teeth, cut a circular plug of flesh, which the shark then swallows.

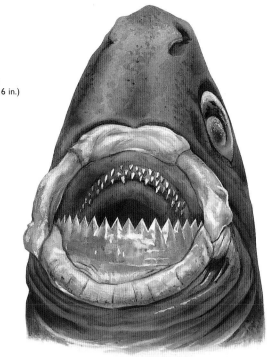

Fact
Cookiecutters mainly take bites out of the bodies of larger fish and marine mammals (like the dolphin in this picture), but there are reports of cookiecutter bite-marks being found on nuclear submarines!

The cookiecutter shark feeds on bites taken from larger sea creatures.

Crocodile shark

The crocodile shark lives in the warmer regions of the open ocean. It is a fast-swimming predator with unusually large eyes. The size of the eyes suggests that it hunts in fairly deep water where there is little light, for prey such as bristlemouths and lanternfishes that glow in the dark water.

Max length:
1 m (3 ft. 3 in.)

Cc

Fact

The crocodile shark gets its name because of its long, spike-like teeth. Its jaws have very powerful muscles, so it can bite very hard. If it is accidently caught in a fishing net, it snaps ferociously, just like a crocodile.

Crown-of-thorns

Max diameter:
80 cm (2 ft. 6 in.)

The crown-of-thorns is the only venomous sea star. It feeds on coral, and in some parts of the world it has been responsible for killing large areas of reef. The crown-of-thorns is covered with spines up to 5 centimetres (2 in.) long. These spines are connected to a network of venom glands in its skin. If you touch a crown-of-thorns starfish the spines can puncture your skin and release toxins that make the skin swell and turn dark blue.

Cuttlefish

Max length:
1 m (3 ft. 3 in.)

The giant Australian cuttlefish is the largest of its kind. It lives in very shallow water, where it feeds on shrimp and crabs. Like other cuttlefish, it has eight ordinary tentacles and two feeding tentacles with hooks for catching prey. It can change the appearance of its skin – to match the seabed for camouflage, or to confuse predators with rapidly changing shapes and colours.

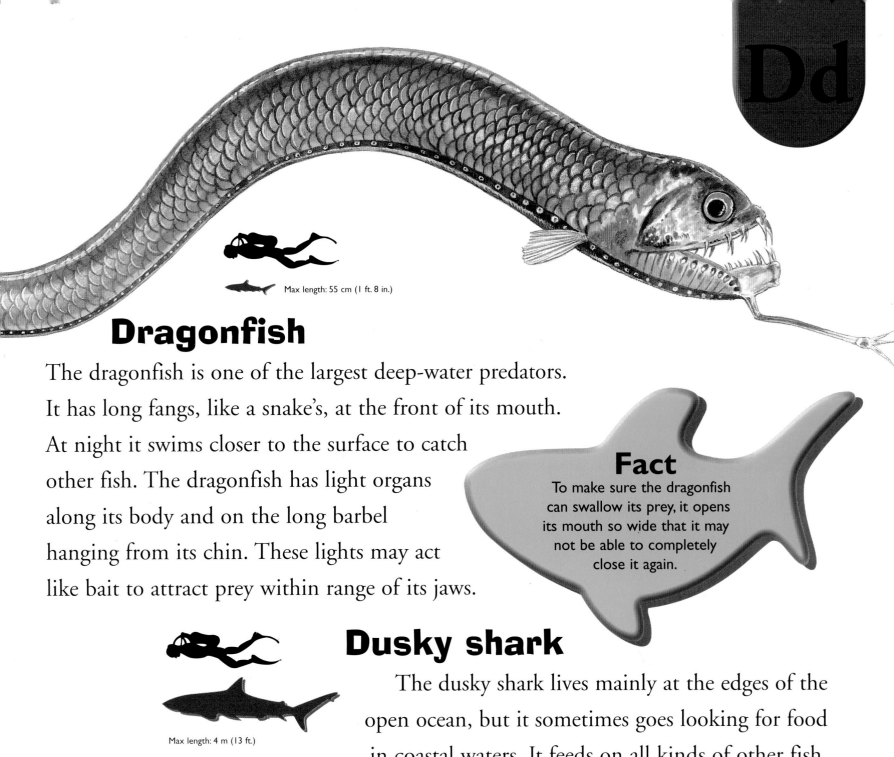

Max length: 55 cm (1 ft. 8 in.)

Dragonfish

The dragonfish is one of the largest deep-water predators. It has long fangs, like a snake's, at the front of its mouth. At night it swims closer to the surface to catch other fish. The dragonfish has light organs along its body and on the long barbel hanging from its chin. These lights may act like bait to attract prey within range of its jaws.

Fact
To make sure the dragonfish can swallow its prey, it opens its mouth so wide that it may not be able to completely close it again.

Dusky shark

Max length: 4 m (13 ft.)

The dusky shark lives mainly at the edges of the open ocean, but it sometimes goes looking for food in coastal waters. It feeds on all kinds of other fish, from small sardines to large tuna. This shark is fast and not a fussy eater, so it is very dangerous for swimmers!

Eagle ray

The eagle ray lives in offshore tropical waters and is a powerful and agile swimmer. It can change direction very quickly to escape from hungry sharks. The eagle ray eats shellfish, using its teeth to crush the hard shells. For defence against sharks, it has a single venomous spine on its tail.

Max width:
3.5 m (11 ft. 5 in.)

Electric ray

Max length:
60 cm (2 ft.)

The electric ray (right) is often found close to the shore, especially during the summer. If you step on one, you will get a shock of up to 80 volts. That is not enough to kill a person, but it might knock you over. The ray generates electric current in banks of special muscle cells along its fins.

Elephant fish

Max length:
1.2 m (4 ft.)

The elephant fish (below) is a chimaera, a type of fish related to sharks. It is also known as the ploughnose chimaera. Both names refer to its unusually long snout. The elephant fish is found in the Southern Hemisphere, mainly in deep water but sometimes closer to the surface.

Max length:
7 m (23 ft.)

Elephant seal

The elephant seal is the biggest seal in the world and the heaviest - one individual weighed about 2700 kilograms (6000 lb). It is a superb underwater predator of fish, but does not attack swimmers or divers. On land, during the mating season, this mammal can be dangerous. The elephant seal will threaten and attack anything, or anybody, that gets too close to its breeding colony.

Fact
Male elephant seals challenge each other for dominance. They bite each other hard on the nose and neck and occasionally one will be killed in the battle.

Epaulette shark

Max length:
1 m 7 cm (5 ft. 6 in.)

The epaulette shark lives in coral reefs around Australia and New Guinea. It hides in shadows during the day and feeds at night. Young epaulette sharks have a striped colouration. The adults are spotted, with a distinctive, large black spot surrounded by white.

Ff

Fire coral

Fire coral is covered with tiny stinging cells and its red colouration serves as a "hands off" warning to all concerned. Many types of coral use stings and other forms of chemical warfare as they struggle with each other for space on a crowded reef. Fire coral is unusual because its stings also affect divers who touch it. The stings can be very painful, and the affected areas may become infected.

Max height: 60 cm (2 ft.)

Fortescue

Max length: 15 cm (6 in.)

The fortescue lives in calm, shallow waters off the coast of Australia. Divers have learned not to touch this small fish. The fortescue has sharp spines on each side of its head, which stick out sideways if the fish is disturbed. It also has another 16 spines along its back.

Foxface

Max length: 25 cm (10 in.)

The foxface is found in the tropical reefs of the Pacific Ocean. It is easily recognised by its elongated snout. The foxface is not a fish to catch in your hands. All of its fins have sharp spines connected to poison glands. The sting is extremely painful.

Frilled shark

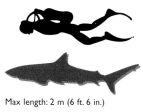

Max length: 2 m (6 ft. 6 in.)

The frilled shark has an eel-like body and frills of skin around its gills. It lives in deep water and only rarely comes near the surface. Each of its teeth has three small, sharp points. These teeth suggest that the frilled shark hunts mainly squid and small fish.

Fact
Even though the frilled shark rarely comes to the surface, scientists suspect it may be the cause of many people reporting sightings of 'sea-serpents' because of its unusual snake-like shape.

Fugu

Max length: 70 cm (2 ft. 3 in.)

The fugu belongs to the group known as blowfish or puffer fish. It has prickles on its skin and can inflate its body with water when frightened. The fugu's flesh is considered a delicacy in Japan, but some of its internal organs are extremely poisonous. If it is not prepared carefully, eating it can kill you!

Max length:
3.6 m (12 ft.)

Galapagos shark

The Galapagos shark is found mainly around tropical islands. It prefers the deeper water at the seaward edges of coral reefs. The Galapagos shark is dangerous and is known to attack swimmers, sometimes with fatal results.

Fact

The Galapagos shark gives birth to up to 16 pups, which are kept in shallow nursery areas to prevent the other adult sharks from eating them!

Max legspan: 17 cm (7 in.)

Ghost crab

The ghost crab sounds scary but it is harmless. It is a small crab that lives in burrows above the high-water mark on sandy beaches. The ghost crab leaves its burrow at night to feed on molluscs and insects. If disturbed, it runs away so quickly that it seems to disappear like a ghost.

Max length: 1.2 m (4 ft.)

Giant clam

The giant clam is the world's heaviest shellfish, a large adult can weigh up to 225 kilograms (500 lb). It lives on tropical reefs in the Pacific Ocean. People used to think that the clam was dangerous and could trap a diver's leg in its huge shell, but this is not true. The giant clam is a harmless creature that is endangered because of overfishing.

Giant Pacific octopus

Max length:
5 m (16 ft.)

The giant Pacific octopus is the largest known octopus and can weigh up to 45 kilograms (100 lb). It lives on the sea bottom in the cooler waters of the northern Pacific. Despite its fearsome appearance, this octopus feeds only on crustaceans and small fish. Females may be aggressive if they are protecting their young.

Fact
To eat shelled prey, the octopus bites the shell open with its beak or uses special saliva that softens the shell to create a tiny hole. Then the octopus releases poison into the hole to paralyse the prey so it can be eaten.

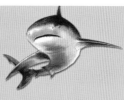

Goblin shark

The goblin shark is one of the strangest of all sharks. It lives in deep water around the edges of the continents. With its mouth closed, the goblin shark looks like a normal shark with a long, pointed snout. When it opens its mouth to seize prey, the goblin shark's jaws project forward viciously, like a pair of toothed pincers.

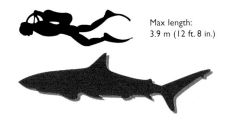

Max length:
3.9 m (12 ft. 8 in.)

Gg

Max length: 1.8 m (6 ft.)

Great torpedo ray

The great torpedo ray is the largest of the electric rays, and can produce shocks of more than 200 volts. It lives in the Atlantic Ocean, and prefers cooler temperate waters. The great torpedo ray spends most of its time on the sea bottom, where it waits to ambush prey such as flatfish and eels. It is not aggressive, and will only attack if provoked or frightened. The electric shock it delivers is powerful enough to stun a person.

Great white shark

Max length:
8 m (26 ft.)

The great white shark is the largest of the predatory sharks, and may be the most dangerous animal in the oceans. It is one of the few sharks known to eat human flesh, and is responsible for most of the unprovoked attacks on swimmers in temperate waters. The great white shark has a fearsome reputation, and poses a real threat to swimmers because it often comes close to the shore in search of prey.

Fact
The great white shark is highly sensitive to any movements in the water made by its prey. If the prey is bleeding, the shark detects its blood from a distance of about 1km (0.6 miles).

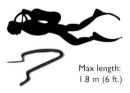

Max length:
1.8 m (6 ft.)

Gulper eel

The gulper eel is one of several deep-sea eels with enormous jaws like a pelican's. It can swallow fish as big as itself. The gulper eel has a light organ at the end of its thin, whip-like tail, which may be used to attract prey.

Hagfish

The hagfish is an eel-shaped, jawless fish. Instead of jaws and teeth, it has pairs of rasps that tear off pieces of flesh, which it swallows. The hagfish feeds by scavenging meat from dead fish and mammals on the sea bottom. If threatened, it produces huge quantities of slime that can suffocate an attacker. For this reason it is also known as the slime eel.

Max length
45 cm (1 ft. 5 in.)

The mouth of the hagfish is surrounded by tentacles.

Max length: 6 m (20 ft.)

Hammerhead shark

The great hammerhead shark is the largest member of a group of sharks that have a unique flattened head. It feeds on fish and rays, which it often catches in shallow water. The hammerhead shark is known to attack people and is considered dangerous, especially to swimmers and reef divers.

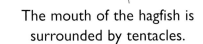

Hh

Hatchet fish

The hatchet fish spends the day in deep water and rises closer to the surface at night to feed. It has light organs on its upper surface to attract small squid and other invertebrates. The hatchet fish also flashes its light organs on and off to communicate with others of its kind.

Max length:
7.5 cm (3 in.)

Hornshark

Max length:
1.2 m (4 ft.)

The hornshark lives in the kelp beds in the shallow waters off the coast of California. It feeds mainly on crabs and sea urchins and is not considered dangerous. The hornshark gets its name from the two horn-like spines in front of its back fins. It belongs to a group of sharks known as the bullhead sharks.

Horseshoe crab

The horseshoe crab usually lives on the sea bottom, but it is sometimes seen on beaches. Although it looks fearsome with its spiny armoured shell and pointed tail, it is harmless and cannot even nip you because it does not have big front pincers like other crabs. In fact, the horseshoe crab is not a true crab, but a distant relative of spiders.

Max length:
60 cm (2 ft.)

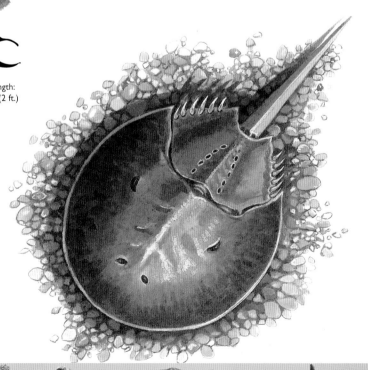

Istiophorus

Istiophorus is also known as the Indo-Pacific sailfish. It is the fastest-swimming fish in the world, and can cut through the water at more than 100 kmph (60 mph) over short distances. The sailfish uses its pointed bill to spear prey and to defend itself against sharks.

Max length: 3 m (10 ft.)

Japanese spider crab

Max legspan: 3.7 m (12 ft.)

The Japanese spider crab is the world's largest arthropod – much bigger than any spider on land. It lives on the seabed around the islands of Japan, and feeds on anything it can reach with its front pincers.

Jellyfish

The lion's mane jelly is one of the world's biggest jellyfish. The largest specimens, with stinging tentacles up to 30 metres (100 ft) long, are found in cold Arctic waters. It does not grow so large in warmer parts of the world. The sting of the lion's mane jelly is strong enough to kill a person.

Max diameter: 2.4 m (8 ft.)

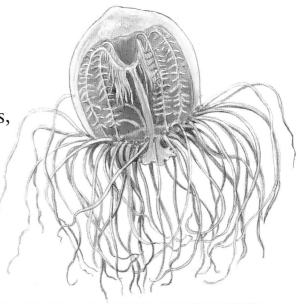

Killer whale

The killer whale is the top ocean predator. It has little to fear from any other sea creature. The killer whale hunts in family groups called pods. It uses echo-location to find prey such as salmon or seals. It also uses bursts of sound to stun, or even kill, its victims.

Max length:
10 m (33 ft.)

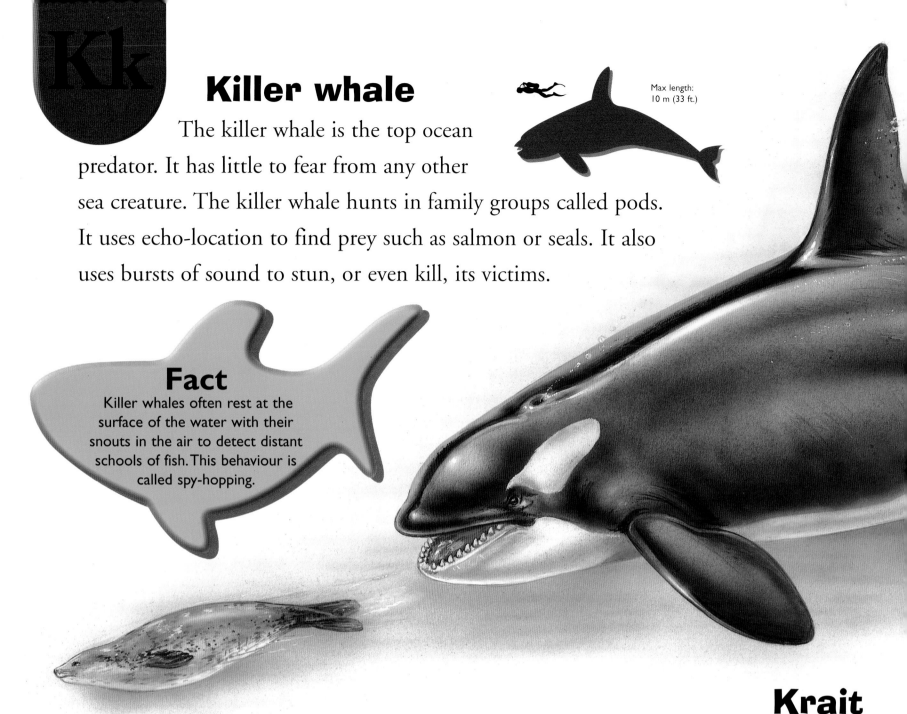

Fact

Killer whales often rest at the surface of the water with their snouts in the air to detect distant schools of fish. This behaviour is called spy-hopping.

Krait

The sea krait is one of about 40 snakes that have adapted to life in the sea. It has a flattened, paddle-shaped body and is an excellent swimmer. The sea krait is extremely venomous, but is not considered dangerous to people because it does not bite. When hunting small fish, it squirts venom into the nearby water to kill its prey.

Max length:
2 m (6 ft. 6 in.)

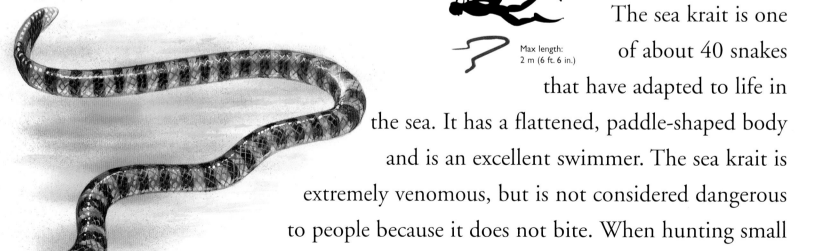

Leech

The marine leech feeds by
attaching itself to the outside of
fish and sucking their blood. It has a sucker
at each end of its worm-like body. The
marine leech has no teeth or jaws;
instead, it has a pointed proboscis
that is projected forward to
pierce its victim's skin.

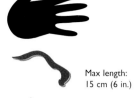

Max length:
15 cm (6 in.)

Max length: 3.4 m (11 ft.)

Lemon shark

The lemon shark lives in the shallow
waters on the landward side of tropical
reefs. It hunts fish, rays
and crustaceans
in beds of sea
grass and around
the roots of
mangrove trees. The
lemon shark can be
dangerous to humans if it is provoked.

Max length:
3.6 m (12 ft.)

Leopard seal

The leopard seal lives in the cold Southern Ocean around the shores of Antarctica. It is a fierce and fast-swimming predator that hunts fish, penguins and other seals. A leopard seal will even crash through thin ice to grab an unwary penguin from below. There have been a few face-to-face encounters between leopard seals and divers in the icy Antarctic waters. So far there are no reports of a leopard seal attacking a person.

Max length: 2.1 m (7 ft.)

Leopard shark

The leopard shark lives along the coasts of California and Oregon in the United States. It has rows of short, sharp teeth and feeds on fish and molluscs. The leopard shark is harmless, but because of its markings it is often mistaken for the dangerous tiger shark. To add to the confusion, the Australian zebra shark is sometimes called the leopard shark.

Lionfish

The lionfish is one of the most deadly fish in the sea. It lives on tropical reefs in the Indian and Pacific Oceans. The lionfish is brightly coloured to warn predators (and divers) not to get too close. Its long, feathery fins are equipped with poisonous spines. Lionfish venom is strong enough to kill a human being.

Max length:
40 cm (1 ft. 3 in.)

Max length:
1 m (3 ft. 3 in.)

Lobster

The lobster has large, powerful pincers, about half the size of its body, that can easily cut off a person's finger. A lobster keeps growing throughout its life and the largest is the American lobster. Because they are such a popular food item, there are very few really big lobsters left in the sea.

Mm

Mako shark

The mako shark is the fastest-swimming shark, and can reach speeds of more than 30 kmph (20 mph). It can also leap 6 metres (20 ft) into the air. The mako shark lives in the open oceans and feeds on fish and squid. It is considered dangerous and has attacked both swimmers and divers.

Max length: 4 m (13 ft.)

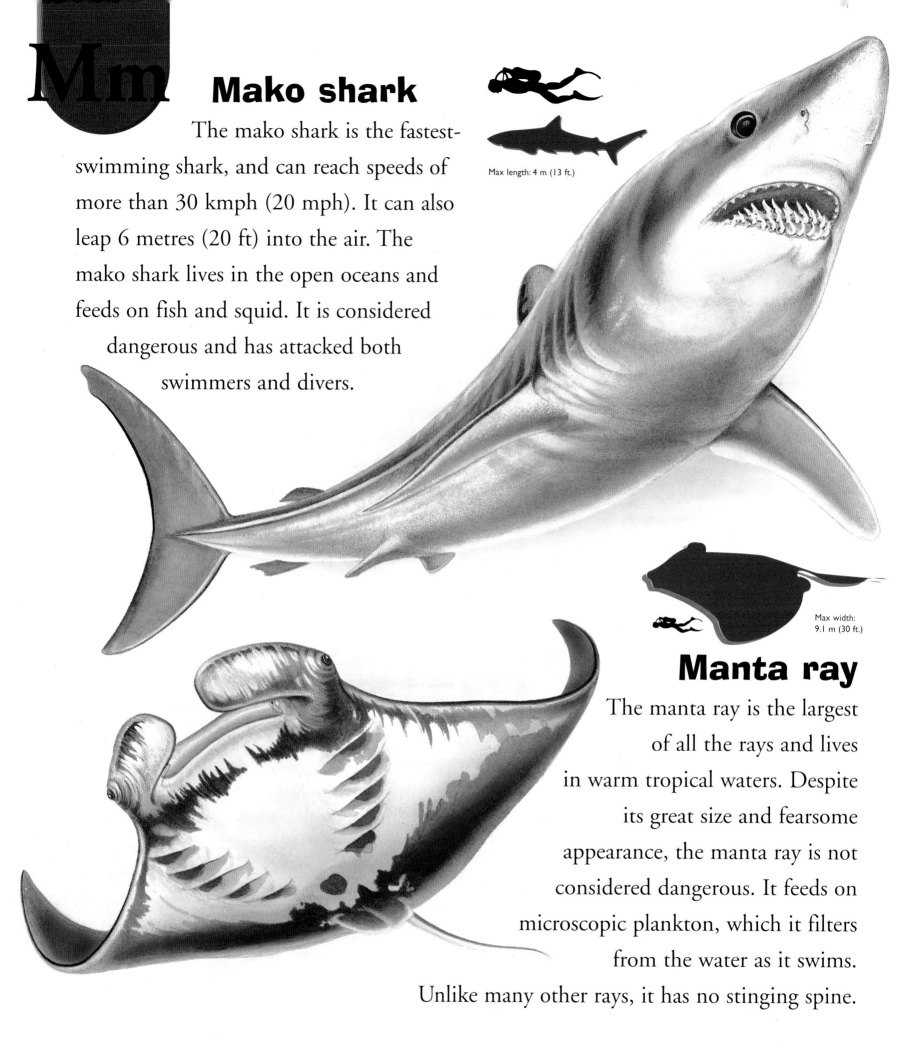

Max width: 9.1 m (30 ft.)

Manta ray

The manta ray is the largest of all the rays and lives in warm tropical waters. Despite its great size and fearsome appearance, the manta ray is not considered dangerous. It feeds on microscopic plankton, which it filters from the water as it swims. Unlike many other rays, it has no stinging spine.

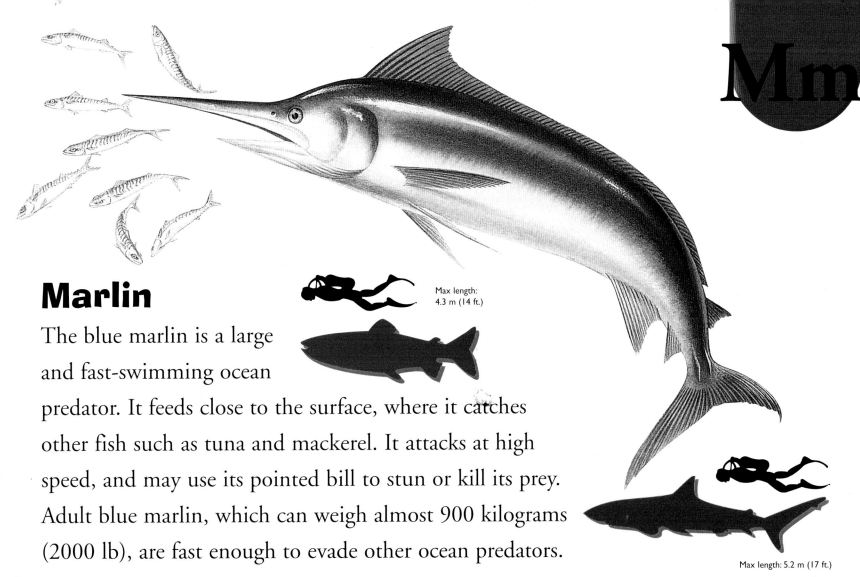

Marlin

The blue marlin is a large and fast-swimming ocean predator. It feeds close to the surface, where it catches other fish such as tuna and mackerel. It attacks at high speed, and may use its pointed bill to stun or kill its prey. Adult blue marlin, which can weigh almost 900 kilograms (2000 lb), are fast enough to evade other ocean predators.

Max length: 4.3 m (14 ft.)

Max length: 5.2 m (17 ft.)

Megamouth shark

The megamouth shark is a rarely seen inhabitant of the ocean depths. It was not discovered until 1976, and there have only been about a dozen sightings. The megamouth shark feeds on small shrimp and other animal plankton, which it gathers in its huge mouth as it swims. It is not considered dangerous because it inhabits waters that are too deep for diving.

Mm Nn

Moray eel

The moray eel is found mainly in tropical and subtropical waters. It has poor eyesight and hunts at night, using its keen sense of smell to find its prey. During the day it shelters in caves and under rocks. If disturbed by a diver, the moray eel can deliver a very nasty bite with its curved and pointed teeth.

Max length:
3 m (10 ft.)

Narwhal

The narwhal is a rare and unique whale that lives in the cold waters around the North Pole. Male narwhals have a long, fierce-looking spiral tusk, which is one greatly extended tooth. The tusk was once believed to be the horn of the fabled unicorn.

Max length:
5 m (16 ft. 4 in.)

Fact
The specific use of the horn is unknown but male narwhals do use their horns to duel with each other in an activity called 'tusking'.

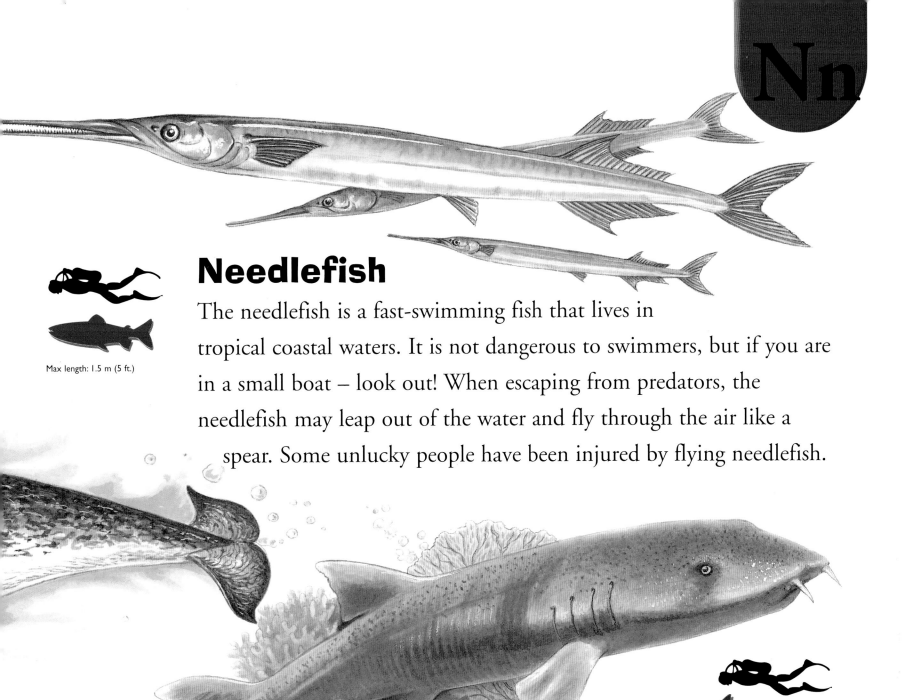

Needlefish

Max length: 1.5 m (5 ft.)

The needlefish is a fast-swimming fish that lives in tropical coastal waters. It is not dangerous to swimmers, but if you are in a small boat – look out! When escaping from predators, the needlefish may leap out of the water and fly through the air like a spear. Some unlucky people have been injured by flying needlefish.

Max length: 4.3 m (14 ft.)

Nurse shark

The nurse shark lives in the shallow tropical and subtropical waters around the coasts of North and South America. It stays close to the sea bottom, where it feeds mainly on crustaceans and molluscs. The nurse shark is a very slow swimmer and can only catch the slowest fish. It can become aggressive if provoked.

Oo

Oarfish

The oarfish is a genuine, but harmless, monster of the deep. It lives in the deep oceans and is only rarely encountered near the surface. Glimpses of its long, silvery body and the crest-like fins on its head may have been the source of some of the sea-serpent legends. It gets its name from the pair of long fins that trail beneath it, like the oars of a rowing boat.

Max length: 8 m (26 ft.)

Max length: 4 m (13 ft.)

Oceanic whitetip shark

The oceanic whitetip shark is a dangerous predator of the warm tropical oceans. Although it is slow-moving, it is aggressive and will attack swimmers or small boats without warning. It is rarely seen near coastlines, and is often confused with the whitetip reef shark, which is smaller, slimmer, and much less dangerous.

Fact
Oceanic whitetip sharks do not come near the shore but have been known to attack and kill people. This is because they take advantage of sea and air disasters, tracking down people struggling in the water.

Pacific sleeper shark

The Pacific sleeper shark inhabits the cold waters of the northern Pacific. It is a deep-water predator that sometimes moves into shallow waters along the coast of Siberia. The Pacific sleeper shark is a slow swimmer, and is not considered dangerous. It feeds mainly on fish and seals.

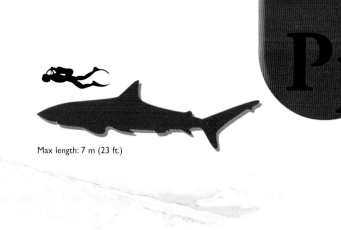

Max length: 7 m (23 ft.)

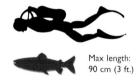

Max length: 90 cm (3 ft.)

Fact
As well as the porcupine fish's spines and its ability to inflate, it can also defend itself by releasing poison into the water to keep enemies away.

Porcupine fish

A porcupine fish can inflate itself with water and increase its size. This makes it much more difficult for a predator to swallow. In addition, porcupine fish are covered with sharp, poisonous spines. Usually, the spines lie along its side, but when the fish inflates itself, the spines stick out in all directions.

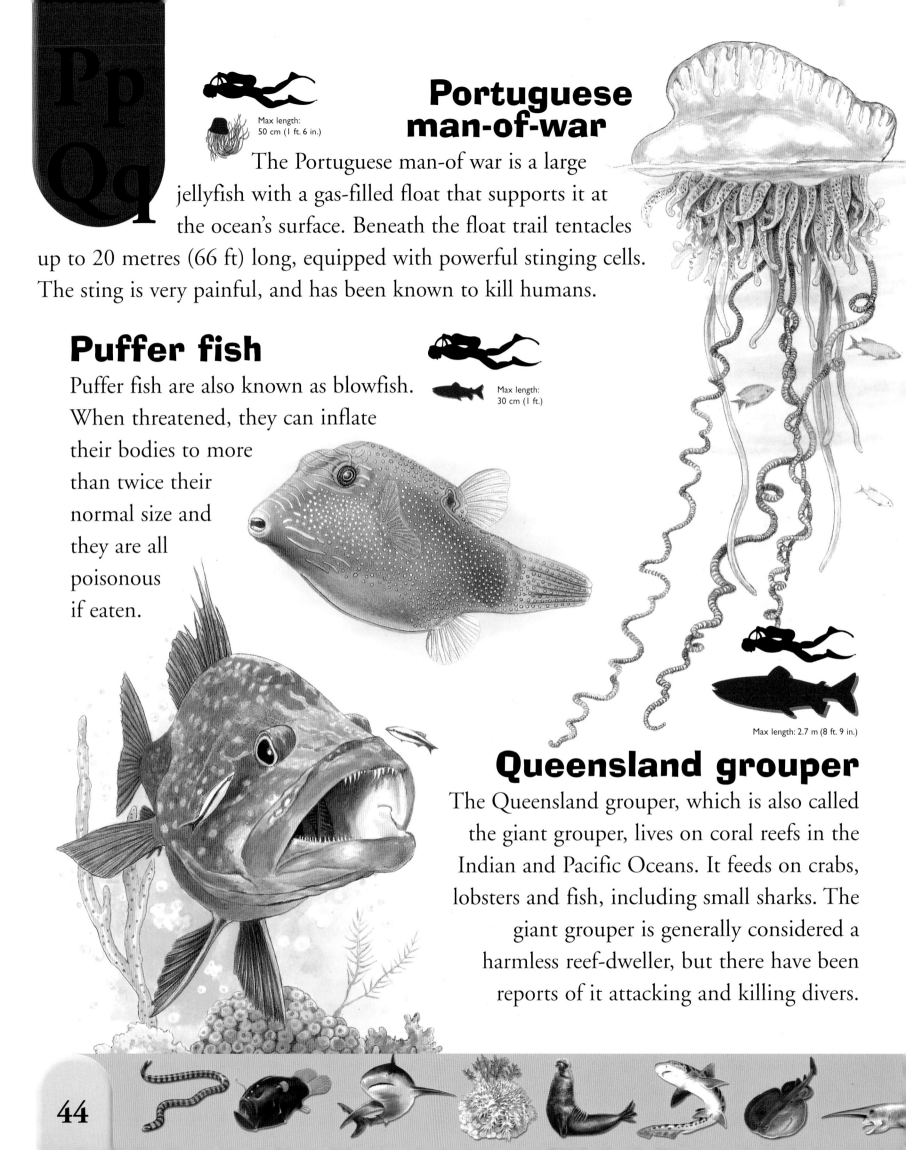

Portuguese man-of-war

Max length:
50 cm (1 ft. 6 in.)

The Portuguese man-of war is a large jellyfish with a gas-filled float that supports it at the ocean's surface. Beneath the float trail tentacles up to 20 metres (66 ft) long, equipped with powerful stinging cells. The sting is very painful, and has been known to kill humans.

Puffer fish

Puffer fish are also known as blowfish. When threatened, they can inflate their bodies to more than twice their normal size and they are all poisonous if eaten.

Max length:
30 cm (1 ft.)

Max length: 2.7 m (8 ft. 9 in.)

Queensland grouper

The Queensland grouper, which is also called the giant grouper, lives on coral reefs in the Indian and Pacific Oceans. It feeds on crabs, lobsters and fish, including small sharks. The giant grouper is generally considered a harmless reef-dweller, but there have been reports of it attacking and killing divers.

Ratfish

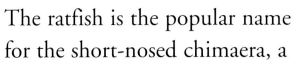

Max length: 1.5 m (5 ft.)

The ratfish is the popular name
for the short-nosed chimaera, a
close relative of the long-nosed elephant fish. It lives
mainly in the ocean depths, but sometimes
swims near the surface in the summer. The
ratfish has a poisonous spine
on its back that can inflict
a painful wound if it is
not handled
with care.

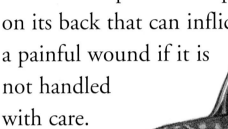

Fact

The ratfish's front teeth are fused
together to form a plate so they
can manage their crunchy diet of
clams and crabs from the ocean
floor. This has earned it the
nickname 'rabbitfish'.

Ribbon worm

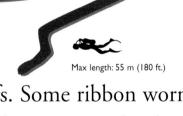

Max length: 55 m (180 ft.)

The ribbon worm is found
in all parts of the sea, but is
most often seen on tropical reefs. Some ribbon worms
are microscopic in size, while others grow to be the
world's longest animals - about twice the length of the
largest whale. The ribbon worm preys on
small invertebrates, but
even the largest
specimens are
harmless to humans.

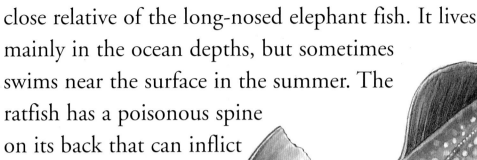

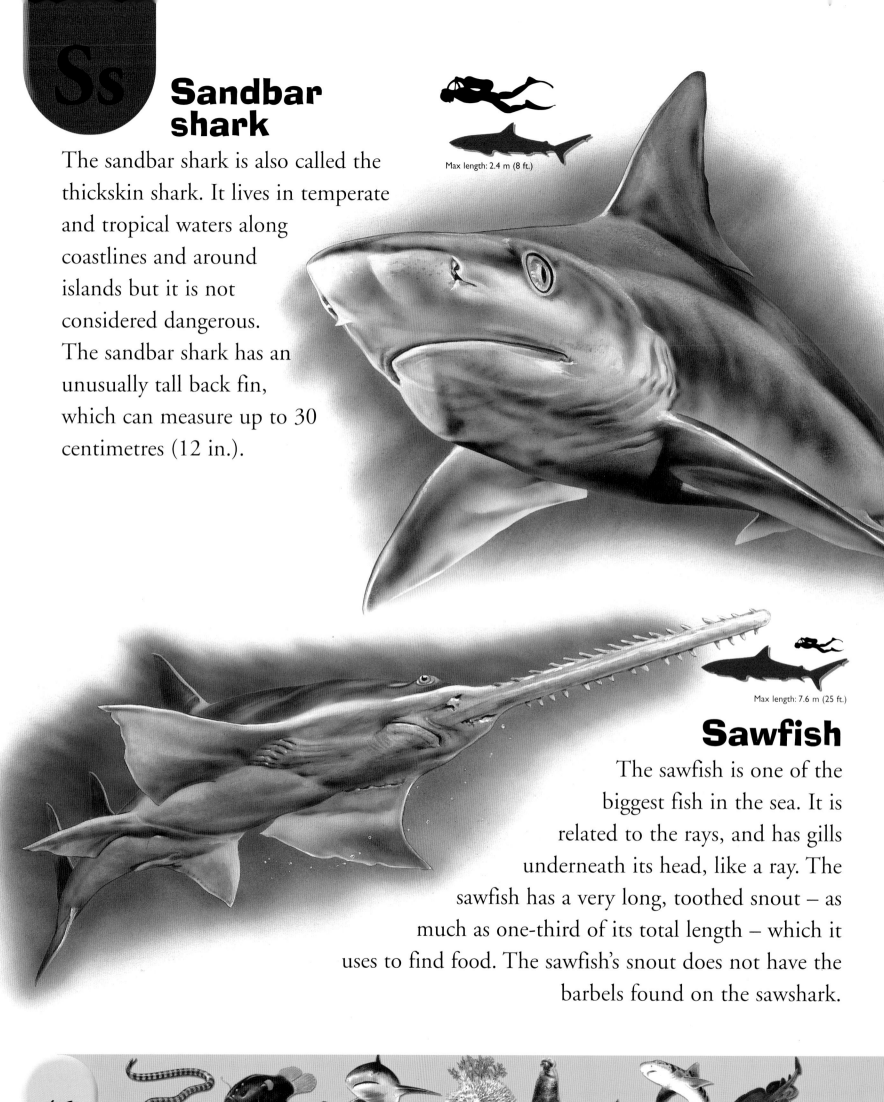

Ss

Sandbar shark

The sandbar shark is also called the thickskin shark. It lives in temperate and tropical waters along coastlines and around islands but it is not considered dangerous. The sandbar shark has an unusually tall back fin, which can measure up to 30 centimetres (12 in.).

Max length: 2.4 m (8 ft.)

Max length: 7.6 m (25 ft.)

Sawfish

The sawfish is one of the biggest fish in the sea. It is related to the rays, and has gills underneath its head, like a ray. The sawfish has a very long, toothed snout – as much as one-third of its total length – which it uses to find food. The sawfish's snout does not have the barbels found on the sawshark.

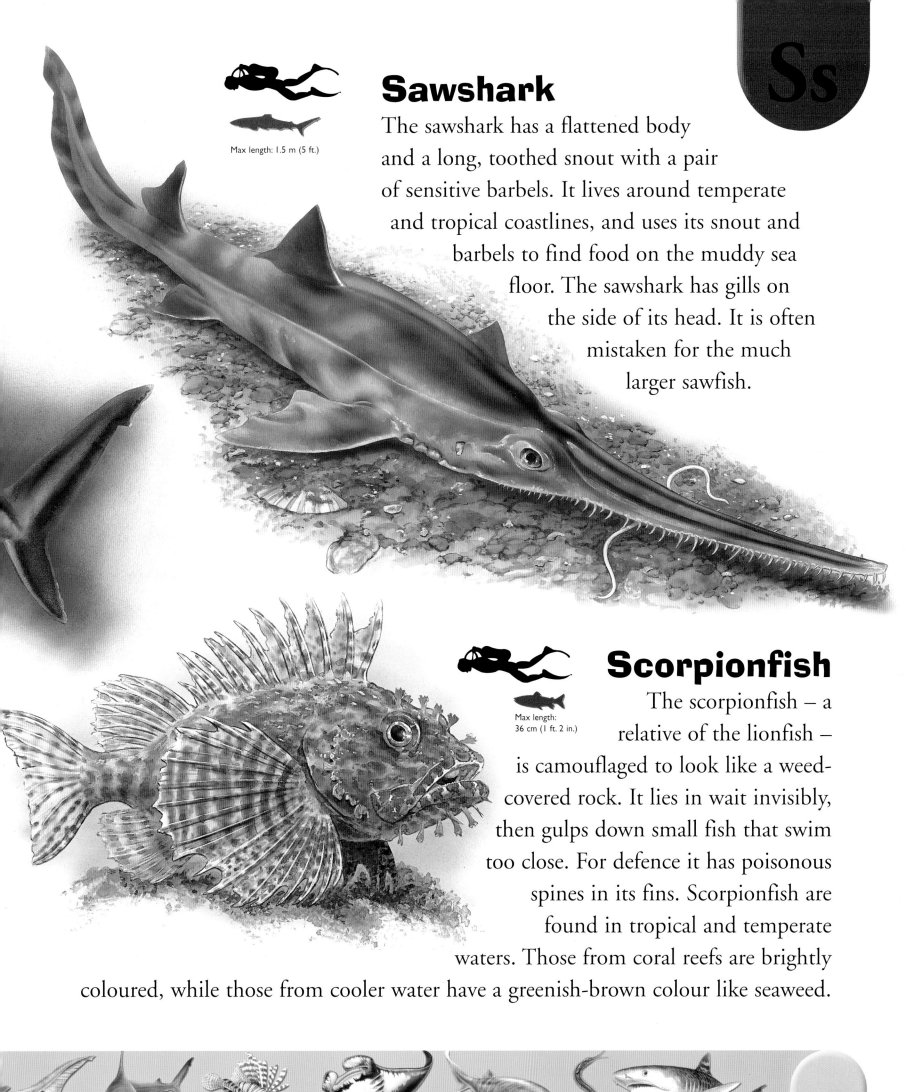

Sawshark

Max length: 1.5 m (5 ft.)

The sawshark has a flattened body and a long, toothed snout with a pair of sensitive barbels. It lives around temperate and tropical coastlines, and uses its snout and barbels to find food on the muddy sea floor. The sawshark has gills on the side of its head. It is often mistaken for the much larger sawfish.

Scorpionfish

Max length: 36 cm (1 ft. 2 in.)

The scorpionfish – a relative of the lionfish – is camouflaged to look like a weed-covered rock. It lies in wait invisibly, then gulps down small fish that swim too close. For defence it has poisonous spines in its fins. Scorpionfish are found in tropical and temperate waters. Those from coral reefs are brightly coloured, while those from cooler water have a greenish-brown colour like seaweed.

Sea cucumber

Max length:
1 m (3 ft. 3 in.)

The sea cucumber is a soft-bodied relative of the sea urchin. It has an elongated body and no hard shell. For defence, the sea cucumber can squirt strands of a poisonous sticky substance from special glands in its body. Some sea cucumbers also have poison in their skin.

Sea lion

Max length:
3.3 m (11 ft.)

The sea lion is a close relative of seals and walruses. It lives in coastal waters and can dive to nearly 90 metres (300 ft) in search of fish such as herring and sardines. When fish are scarce, it will catch sea birds at the surface, or hunt for young seals. Its strong whiskers may help it to detect movement in the water to track down prey.

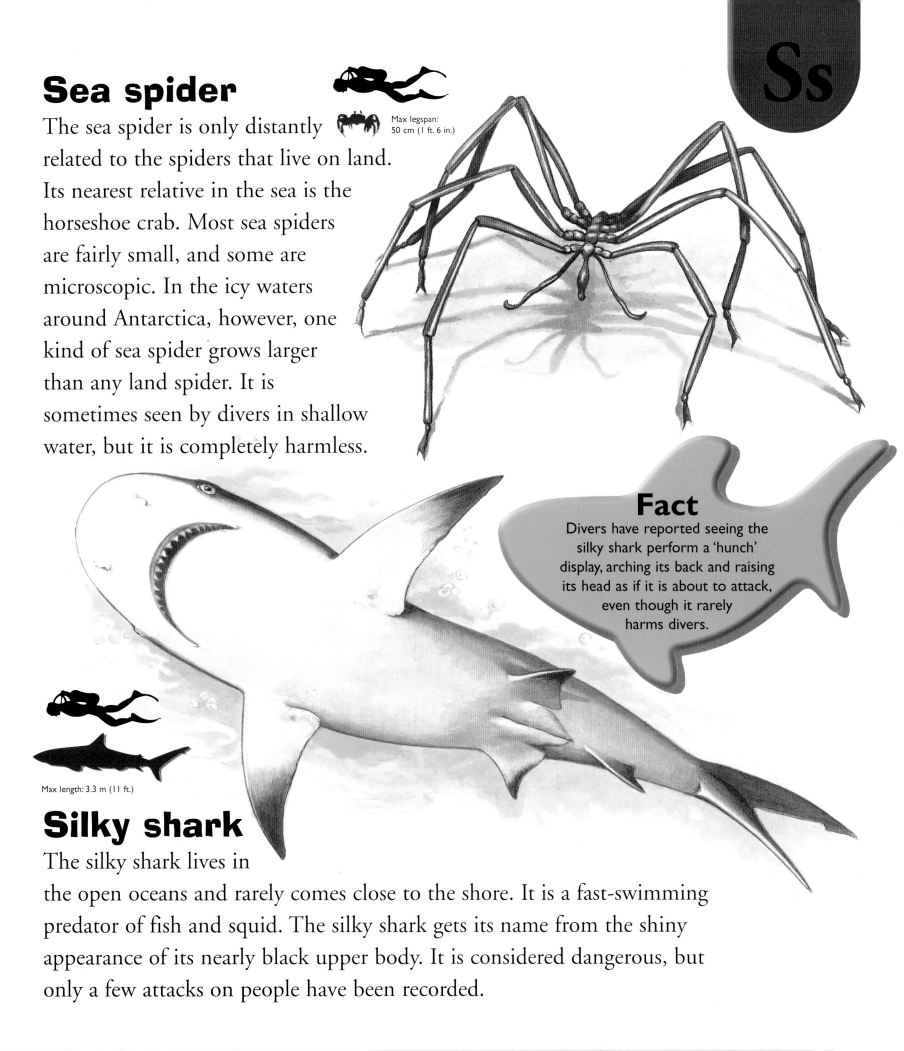

Sea spider

The sea spider is only distantly related to the spiders that live on land. Its nearest relative in the sea is the horseshoe crab. Most sea spiders are fairly small, and some are microscopic. In the icy waters around Antarctica, however, one kind of sea spider grows larger than any land spider. It is sometimes seen by divers in shallow water, but it is completely harmless.

Max legspan: 50 cm (1 ft. 6 in.)

Fact
Divers have reported seeing the silky shark perform a 'hunch' display, arching its back and raising its head as if it is about to attack, even though it rarely harms divers.

Max length: 3.3 m (11 ft.)

Silky shark

The silky shark lives in the open oceans and rarely comes close to the shore. It is a fast-swimming predator of fish and squid. The silky shark gets its name from the shiny appearance of its nearly black upper body. It is considered dangerous, but only a few attacks on people have been recorded.

Ss

Snipe eel

Max length:
75 cm (2 ft. 5 in.)

The snipe eel is a deep-sea eel with elongated jaws and a thin, whip-like tail. The jaws curve outward and do not shut completely. The snipe eel feeds on shrimp, which it catches by hanging vertically, head down, in the water.

Sperm whale

Max length: 20 m (66 ft.)

The sperm whale is by far the largest of the toothed whales. A fully grown male can weigh more than 50 tonnes. The sperm whale feeds mainly on squid, which it hunts in deep water. The sperm whale is not considered dangerous, but it can easily overturn small boats.

Squid

The mysterious giant squid is the world's largest invertebrate, and one of the largest animals in the sea. Only a few dead specimens have been studied, and no giant squid has yet been caught alive. Scientists believe that it lives in deep water and rarely comes near the surface.

Max length: 18 m (59 ft.)

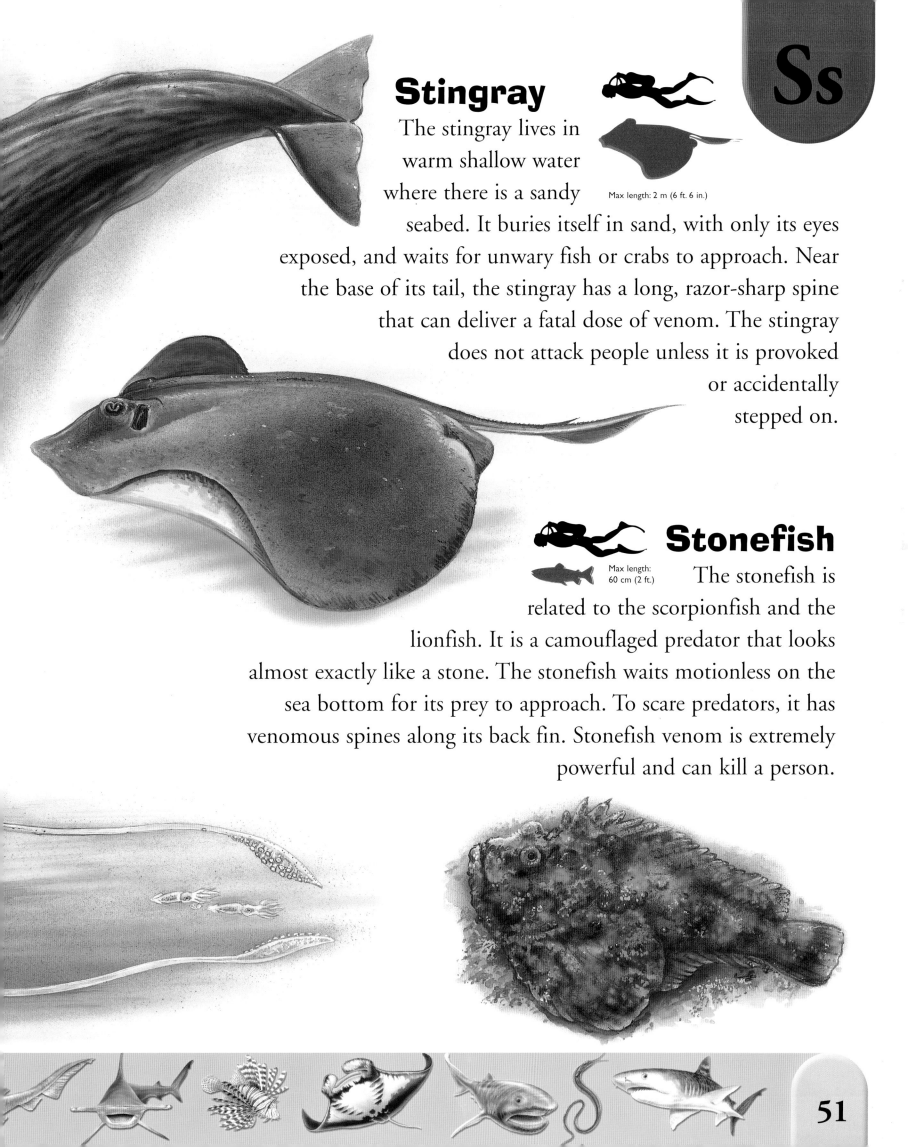

Stingray

Max length: 2 m (6 ft. 6 in.)

The stingray lives in warm shallow water where there is a sandy seabed. It buries itself in sand, with only its eyes exposed, and waits for unwary fish or crabs to approach. Near the base of its tail, the stingray has a long, razor-sharp spine that can deliver a fatal dose of venom. The stingray does not attack people unless it is provoked or accidentally stepped on.

Stonefish

Max length: 60 cm (2 ft.)

The stonefish is related to the scorpionfish and the lionfish. It is a camouflaged predator that looks almost exactly like a stone. The stonefish waits motionless on the sea bottom for its prey to approach. To scare predators, it has venomous spines along its back fin. Stonefish venom is extremely powerful and can kill a person.

Ss

Max length:
4.5 m (15 ft.)

Sunfish

The sunfish, with its huge, disc-shaped body and long fins, is the world's heaviest bony fish. Adults can weigh more than 2 tonnes. The sunfish lives in the open ocean, and often feeds near the surface. Despite its great bulk, it can leap out of the water if it is alarmed.

Swordfish

Max length: 4.5 m (15 ft.)

The swordfish is a large, fast-swimming predator of the open oceans, where it hunts fish and squid. It uses its flattened 'sword' to slash its prey into pieces that can be swallowed easily. Swordfish are aggressive and sometimes attack small boats with sufficient force to break right through the hull.

Thresher shark

The thresher shark is identifiable by its elongated tail. The shark uses its tail to slap the water and frighten fish, herding them into small groups that are easy to catch. The thresher shark is not aggressive to people, but care should be taken to keep clear of its powerful tail.

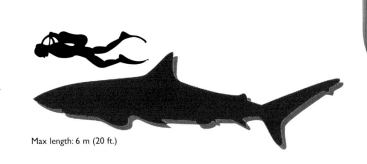

Max length: 6 m (20 ft.)

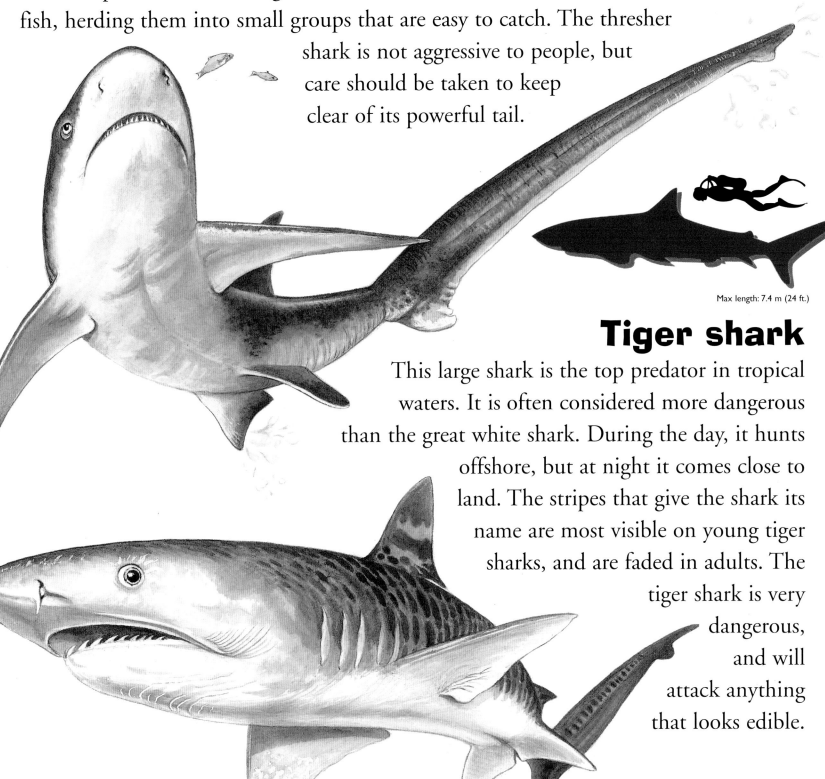

Max length: 7.4 m (24 ft.)

Tiger shark

This large shark is the top predator in tropical waters. It is often considered more dangerous than the great white shark. During the day, it hunts offshore, but at night it comes close to land. The stripes that give the shark its name are most visible on young tiger sharks, and are faded in adults. The tiger shark is very dangerous, and will attack anything that looks edible.

Tt

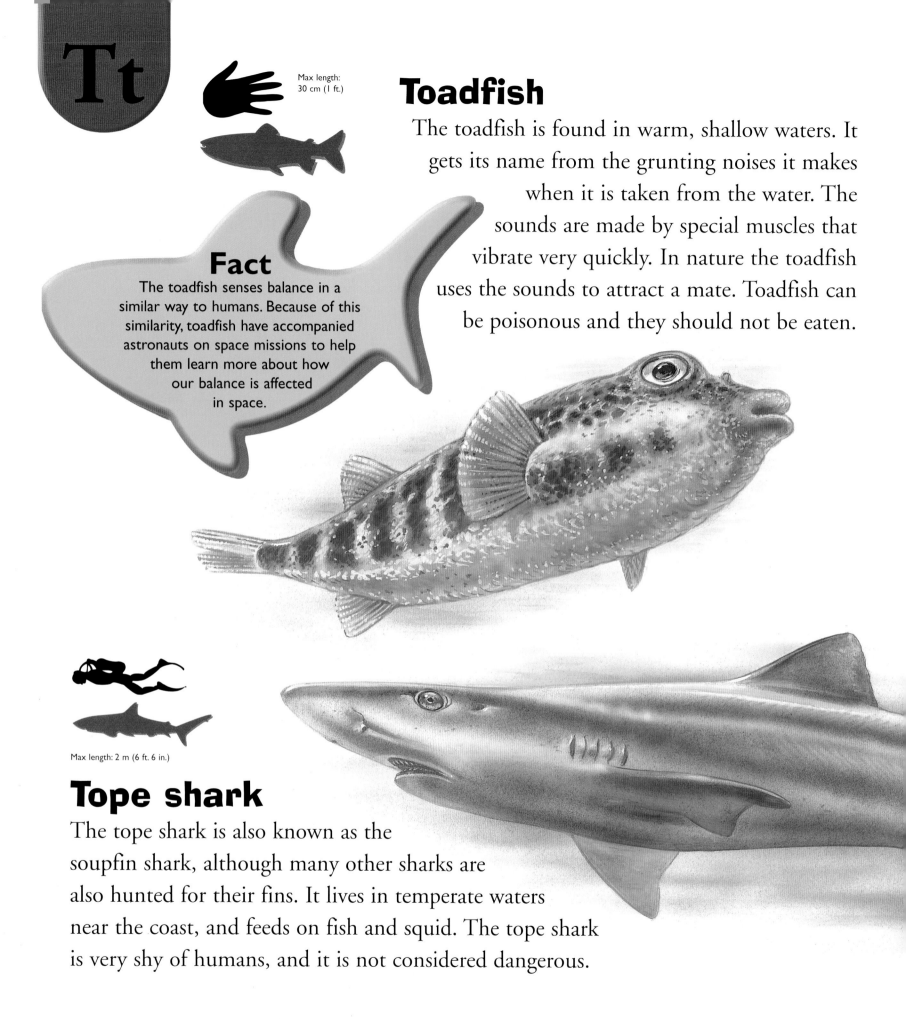

Max length:
30 cm (1 ft.)

Toadfish

The toadfish is found in warm, shallow waters. It gets its name from the grunting noises it makes when it is taken from the water. The sounds are made by special muscles that vibrate very quickly. In nature the toadfish uses the sounds to attract a mate. Toadfish can be poisonous and they should not be eaten.

Fact

The toadfish senses balance in a similar way to humans. Because of this similarity, toadfish have accompanied astronauts on space missions to help them learn more about how our balance is affected in space.

Max length: 2 m (6 ft. 6 in.)

Tope shark

The tope shark is also known as the soupfin shark, although many other sharks are also hunted for their fins. It lives in temperate waters near the coast, and feeds on fish and squid. The tope shark is very shy of humans, and it is not considered dangerous.

Max length:
1m (3 ft. 3 in.)

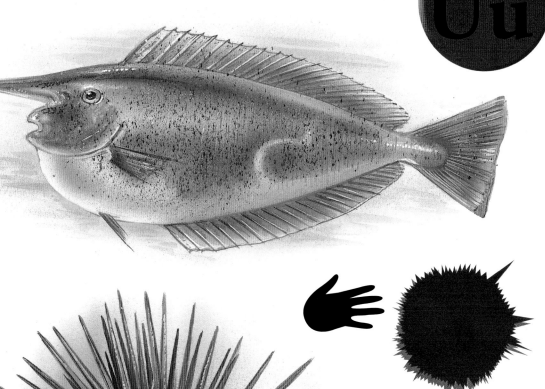

Unicornfish

The unicornfish gets its name from the horn-like projection at the front of its head. It lives around coral reefs in the Pacific Ocean, where it feeds on crustaceans. The unicornfish does not use its strange horn for fighting, but it has razor-sharp spines in its tail for defence.

Max length: 35 cm (1 ft. 1 in.)

Urchin

The sea urchin is a relative of the starfish, and lives around reefs and on the seabed. It has a ball-shaped shell that is covered with sharp spines. If the urchin is handled or stepped on, a spine can pierce human flesh, causing a painful wound. Some sea urchins that live in tropical waters have venomous spines that inject poison.

Vv

Max length: 5 cm (2 in.)

Vampire squid

The vampire squid lives in deep tropical waters and has the most alarming appearance of any sea creature. Eight of its tentacles are webbed together and have jagged spines along the underside. When the vampire squid is threatened, its pulls back its tentacles and envelops itself with a spiny hood.

Fact

The vampire squid is actually neither a vampire nor a true squid! It has its own family name, Vampyromorpha. The name comes from its appearance, with webbing between its tentacles, just like the wings of a vampire bat.

Viperfish

Max length: 35 cm (1 ft. 1 in.)

The viperfish is a deep-sea predator with long, needle-sharp teeth that are too big to fit inside its mouth. The teeth are transparent, like glass, but very strong. The viperfish can open its jaws extremely wide to seize prey, impaling its victims on its curved fangs.

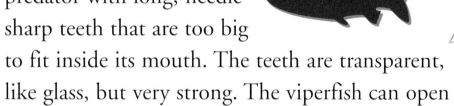

Walrus

The walrus, a close relative of the seals, lives in and around the Arctic Ocean. An adult male can weigh up to 2 tonnes and have tusks measuring 1 metre (3 ft. 3 in.) long. The tusks are actually a pair of extended upper teeth, and are used for fighting between males.

Max length: 3.6 m (12 ft.)

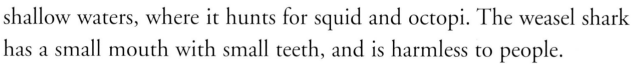

Weasel shark

The weasel shark lives around tropical coastlines, mainly in the Pacific Ocean. It prefers shallow waters, where it hunts for squid and octopi. The weasel shark has a small mouth with small teeth, and is harmless to people.

Max length: 1.4 m (4 ft. 6 in.)

Weeverfish

The weeverfish lives in temperate coastal waters. It spends much of the time buried in sand or mud with only its eyes and back fin showing. Waders often step on weeverfish – with painful and dangerous results. Along its back fin, the weeverfish has a row of venomous spines. The venom can cause human victims to become unconscious, and perhaps drown.

Max length: 20 cm (8 in.)

Whale shark

Max length: 14 m (46 ft.)

The whale shark is the world's biggest fish, and a fully grown adult can weigh more than 12 tonnes. Despite its great size, this giant shark is completely harmless and feeds mainly on plankton. Its enormous mouth, which can be up to 1 metre (3 ft. 3 in.) across, is equipped with extremely small teeth.

Max length: 3 m (10 ft.)

Wobbegong shark

The wobbegong is a shark found in the Pacific Ocean, especially around Australia, where it is fairly common in shallow waters. It has a flattened, camouflaged body and irregular barbels around its mouth. The wobbegong waits on the seabed to seize any prey that swims too close. The tasselled wobbegong is responsible for killing a number of people in Papua New Guinea.

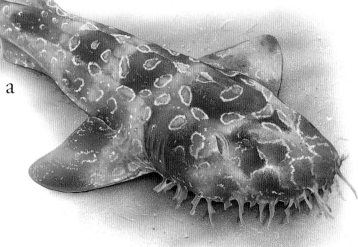

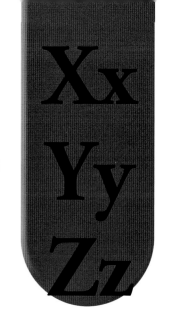

Xenocongrid eel

Max length:
20 cm (8 in.)

The xenocongrid eel lives around a few isolated islands in the Indian and Pacific Oceans. It is also known as the false moray eel. Both its names are confusing, because it is not an eel. The xenocongrid eel is actually a fish with a very eel-like body.

Yellow-eyed surgeonfish

Max length: 18 cm (7 in.)

The yellow-eyed surgeonfish lives on tropical reefs in the Indian and Pacific Oceans. It feeds on small plants, which it combs off rocks with its bristle-like teeth. The surgeonfish gets its name from the sharp, knife-like spines at the base of its tail. By flicking its tail from side to side, it can slash a predator's mouth and head.

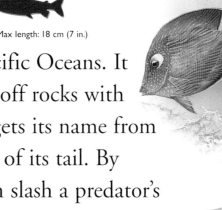

Zebra shark

Max length: 3.5 m (11 ft. 5 in.)

The zebra shark is a slow-moving inhabitant of tropical reefs in the Indian and Pacific Oceans. It is harmless and feeds mainly on crustaceans. Because of its pattern and colouration, the zebra shark is often mistakenly called the leopard shark.

Glossary

Arthropod An invertebrate animal that has an outer casing and several pairs of jointed legs. Insects, spiders and crustaceans are all arthropods.

Barbel A short, fleshy growth located near the mouths of some fish. Barbels are sense organs – sensitive to both touch and taste – that are used to detect food.

Bill The hard, extended jaws of fish such as the marlin and swordfish (and also the beak of a bird).

Bivalve A mollusc, such as the clam, that has two shells (scientifically known as valves) that are joined by a hinge.

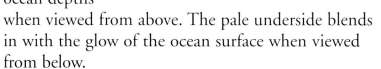

Bony fish A fish with a skeleton made of bone. Most fish are bony fish, but sharks, rays and chimaeras have skeletons made of cartilage.

Camouflage Shape, colour, and pattern that help an animal blend in with its background, so that its enemies – and its prey – cannot see it easily.

Cartilage Very tough, flexible body material. In most vertebrates, cartilage joins bones together, but sharks and their relatives have skeletons that are made entirely of cartilage.

Chimaera A type of mainly deep-sea fish related to sharks and rays.

Cnidaria The scientific name for the group of invertebrates that includes jellyfish, anemones and coral animals. Cnidarians have soft bodies and stinging tentacles.

Coral Limestone structures formed over many years by tiny animals that make protective limestone cups for themselves. Millions of coral animals live side by side on the outer surface of coral.

Countershading A type of camouflage that makes the upper side of a fish dark-coloured, while the underside is pale. The dark colouring makes the fish hard to see against the dark ocean depths when viewed from above. The pale underside blends in with the glow of the ocean surface when viewed from below.

Countershading on the eagle ray

Crustacean A type of arthropod that is found almost exclusively in the sea. Crabs, shrimps and lobsters are all crustaceans.

Deep water In the sea, deep water means more than 200 metres (660 ft) deep, and some animals live at depths of 2000 metres (6600 ft) or more.

Echinoderm A sea animal that has a tough outer shell and moves around on flexible sucker-feet. Starfish and sea urchins are some of the most common types of echinoderm.

Echo-location A method of detecting prey used by dolphins and whales. The animal sends out bursts of sound and uses the echoes to locate its prey.

Glossary

Eel A type of bony fish that has a slim, elongated body and very small fins.

Fin A body part that projects from the back or sides of a fish. Most fish have at least three fins, one running above the backbone, and one on each side of the body. Most bony fish have fragile fins that are stiffened by rays of hard material. Sharks' fins are covered with the same tough skin as their bodies. Rays do not have normal fins, but have developed muscular 'wings'. The projection on the back of a whale or dolphin is known as its fin; those at its side are called flippers.

Flatfish Popular name for bony fish that have flattened bodies and live on the seabed. Flatfish look like other fish when they are young and flatten out as they get older, unlike rays, which keep the same shape throughout their lives.

Fresh water Rainwater, river water, and the water in most lakes is called fresh water because it contains no salt. Seawater is very salty and also contains other dissolved substances.

Gastropod The scientific name for a snail or slug, both of which are types of mollusc.

Gills The organs that fish, and some other sea creatures, use to breathe under water. In most fish, the gills are visible as slits on the sides of the head, behind the jaws. Some fish use their gills to filter food from water taken in by the mouth.

Gland A small organ that produces chemicals needed by an animal. Many sea animals have glands that produce toxins and venom.

Invertebrate An animal that does not have an internal skeleton with a backbone. Arthropods, echinoderms, molluscs, cnidarians and worms are all types of invertebrate.

Jawless fish A small group of fish, which includes the hagfish, that do not have normal vertebrate jaws, but instead have circular mouths with rasping plates instead of teeth.

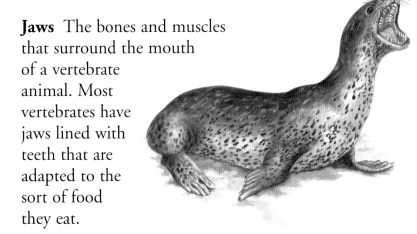

Jaws The bones and muscles that surround the mouth of a vertebrate animal. Most vertebrates have jaws lined with teeth that are adapted to the sort of food they eat.

Juvenile An animal that is not fully grown.

Kelp A seaweed that grows long strands anchored to the sea bottom. Along some coasts, kelp forms 'forests' that attract many sea creatures.

Lure A fleshy stalk growing from a fish's head and dangling near its mouth. A lure is intended to attract prey, and deep-sea predators often have glowing lures.

Mammal A warm-blooded vertebrate animal that produces live-born young. There are relatively few types of mammal that live in the sea, and these include whales, dolphins and seals

Mangrove A tropical tree that can survive with its roots in very shallow salt water. Mangrove forests grow along many tropical coastlines, and provide a rich source of food for sea creatures.

Mollusc A soft-bodied invertebrate animal. Some molluscs, for example bivalves and some gastropods, make hard, protective shells for themselves. Another group of molluscs, which includes octopi and squid, have no external shell, and are equipped with long, grasping tentacles.

Organ Part of an animal's body that does a special job. For example, lungs (in mammals) and gills (in fish) are organs for breathing.

Overfishing When more fish are caught than are left to grow to adulthood each year, so that the total number of fish in the sea decreases. Some sharks and other sea creatures are threatened by extinction because of overfishing.

Oxygen The chemical gas in air, which is essential for living things. Land animals take in oxygen directly from the air. Fish and most other sea creatures extract oxygen that is dissolved in seawater.

Pincers Hinged body parts at the end of most crustacean limbs. The pincers are used for grasping and cutting.

Pod A family group of whales or dolphins.

Poison A substance that can cause injury, sickness, or even death.

Plankton Tiny water animals and plants that range in size from the microscopic to about 2.5 centimetres (1 in.) in length. Much of the animal plankton consists of hatchlings and the juvenile stages of fish and other sea animals. Plant plankton is an important source of both food and oxygen.

Predator An animal that hunts other animals to eat.

Prey An animal that is hunted and eaten by others.

Proboscis The extendable mouthpart used by many invertebrates while feeding. The term is also applied to the elephant's trunk, and even to the human nose.

Ray A type of fish, related to sharks, that has a skeleton made of cartilage, and a very flat body. Many rays have a whip-like tail with sharp spines.

Reef An expanse of rock just below the surface of the sea in coastal waters. Most reefs are coral reefs, which have been built up over thousands of years from the remains of coral animals. Coral reefs have a surface layer of living coral animals, and are found only in tropical and subtropical regions.

Reptile A cold-blooded vertebrate that breathes air and produces eggs with tough, leathery shells. Among the very few reptiles that live in the ocean are some sea turtles and sea snakes.

Glossary

Saliva A clear liquid made in the mouth that helps digest food.

Sea grass A plant that grows in shallow water where the seabed is sandy. Sea grass is not a seaweed, but a flowering plant, like most land plants.

Scales Small, disc-like plates that protect the skin of many fish.

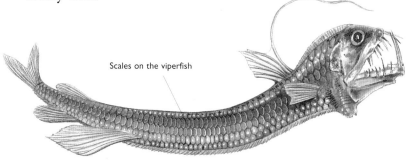

Scales on the viperfish

Shallow water In the sea, shallow water ranges from ankle-depth to about 30 metres (110 ft.) deep.

Shark A type of fish with a skeleton made of cartilage, and tough skin without scales. All sharks are predators, although some eat only invertebrates, and many have powerful jaws with very sharp teeth.

Shellfish A non-scientific term for invertebrate sea creatures, such as crustaceans, urchins and bivalve molluscs, that have a hard outer shell.

Silhouette The shape made by an animal or object when it is viewed against a bright background.

Skeleton The internal framework of bones or cartilage that gives shape and strength to the bodies of vertebrate animals. The outer covering of arthropods is called the exoskeleton (external skeleton).

Snout The foremost part of an animal's head, usually the part just above, or around, the mouth.

Subtropical Belonging to the geographical regions on either side of the tropical zone.

Temperate Moderate – temperate regions have warm summers and cool winters, and occur between the subtropics and the poles.

Tentacle The long, boneless limb of a non-arthropod invertebrate. Tentacles are used for catching prey and are often equipped with suckers.

Toxin Any poison produced inside the body of a living thing. The word 'toxic' is often used to mean poisonous.

Tropical Belonging to the geographical region around the equator, between the Tropic of Cancer and the Tropic of Capricorn.

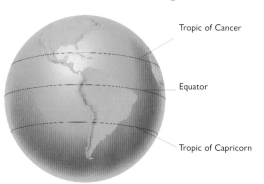

Tropic of Cancer

Equator

Tropic of Capricorn

Venom A poison produced by an animal for the specific purpose of injuring another animal.

Vertebrate An animal that has an internal skeleton arranged around a backbone. Fish, reptiles and mammals are all vertebrates.

Index